Y-TRAIL PROGRAMS MANUAL

Y-TRAIL PROGRAMS MANUAL

YMCA of the USA

Cover Design: Paul Fitzgerald

Copyright © 1987 YMCA of the USA
Published for the YMCA of the USA by Human Kinetics Publishers, Inc.

ISBN: 0-87322-117-6

All rights reserved. Except for use in a review, the reproduction or utilization of this work in any form or by any electronic, mechanical, or other means, now known or hereafter invented, including xerography, photocopying, and recording, and in any information storage and retrieval system, is forbidden without the written permission of the publisher.

The YMCA of the USA does not operate any trail programs.

Printed in the United States of America   10   9   8   7   6

Copies of this book may be purchased from the YMCA Program Store, P.O Box 5076, Champaign, IL 61825-5076, 1-800-747-0089.

Y-Trail Programs

PURPOSE

The purpose of the Y-Trail Programs is to foster a healthy relationship between parent and child built on trust, companionship, understanding, and communication.

MOTTO

"Parent and child, blazing new trails together."

THE AIMS

1. To strengthen the bonds of companionship with my (father/mother/son/daughter).
2. To increase in fitness, physical skills, and body development.
3. To grow in wisdom, intellectual curiosity, and independence.
4. To develop reverence for the Creator, spiritual understanding, and faith for daily living.
5. To serve others, young and old, who are in need, sick, or lonely.
6. To gain in appreciation, love, and support of my family.

PLEDGE

"As a Y-Trail (Blazer/Mate/Maiden), my pledge is to strengthen the bonds of companionship with my (father/mother/son/daughter) as we explore our environment, our community, and our lives together, seeking to grow in spiritual, mental, and physical fitness, and in service to others."

Contents

Foreword ix

Acknowledgments xi

Chapter 1 Introduction   1
Basic Information   2
History of Y-Trail Programs   2
Differences Between Indian Guide and Trail Programs   2
Emblem   3
Themes   4
Group Procedure and Officers   4

Chapter 2 Program and Group Planning Tools   7
Starting a Y-Trail Program   7
Facilitating Skills   8
Brainstorming, Storyboarding, and Creativity   10

Chapter 3 Child and Parent Development   13
Developmental Tasks of 9- to 12-Year-Olds   13
A Word About the Teen Years   15

Chapter 4 Activities   17
Group Meetings   17
Family Activities   18
Outings   18
Special Interest Group Meetings   19
Parent/Child Communication Activities   19

Chapter 5 Recognition and Awards   21
The National Award System   21
Record Keeping, Monitoring, and Procedures   22
Award Requirements   22

Chapter 6 Y-Trail Programs and the YMCA   39

Appendix   41
Y-Trail Programs Sample Planning Calendar   42
Y-Trail Programs Roster   43

Foreword

Why do parents and children join Y-Indian Guide Programs? Is it something magical? Yes, say the many millions of families who have been involved in these programs for more than 60 years!

It is magic when parents and their children are having fun together—laughing, loving, growing, and learning together. These are memories that will last at least two lifetimes, and they can form a meaningful relationship that can last forever.

But for those who have completed two or three years of Y-Indian Guide Programs and want to continue, there is a way to do so—through the Y-Trail Programs, formally referred to as Trail Blazers. The Y-Trail Programs make it possible for the father-son, father-daughter, mother-son, mother-daughter relationships to continue but in a different way, recognizing the psychological needs of 9 to 11 year olds. Y-Trail Programs are aimed at helping the developing child grow toward independence without losing sight of the interdependence of family members. In these programs the youngsters take on more of a leadership role and greater responsibility for the programs. Parents who participate learn to appreciate their own changing roles as their children grow older.

This handbook has been created by experienced participants in Y-Trail Programs to help group leaders and Y staff members start and operate their own Y-Trail Programs. After an introduction explaining the programs, there are chapters on program and group planning and on child and parent development. These are followed by suggested activities for group members and their families. Next is an explanation of the national award system for completing projects in specialized areas of interest and a listing of the award requirements. The book ends with a short section on the relationship of the YMCA to the Y-Trail Programs. In the appendix are a helpful sample planning calendar and a program roster. Hopefully, this handbook will provide the information needed for many more parents and children to find and enjoy the fun, closeness, and growth possible through the Y-Trail Programs.

Acknowledgments

We are grateful to the special task force that developed a large share of the material found in this manual. The task force was chaired by Victoria Dolton, Michigan, and included G. Robert Rank, Ohio; "Jim Bob" Price, Arkansas; and Paul Fitzgerald, Connecticut. All of them have been very active in their local YMCA programs and all have served as regional chiefs; Rank, Price, and Fitzgerald are past national chiefs as well.

We want to acknowledge the work of Robert Phipps, YMCA Metropolitan staff member, Toledo, Ohio, who wrote much of this manual. Before the final printing and editing, the material was also reviewed by the National Program Council of the National Longhouse.

Chapter 1

Introduction

YMCA Trail Programs are a continuation for older children of the YMCA Indian Guide Programs, which are designed for young children and their parents. Y-Indian Guide Programs provide small groups of six- to eight-year-old children and their parents with opportunities to develop companionship and understanding through fun projects and activities based on Indian themes. The Trail Programs offer children nine and over more challenging and varied experiences. Four Trail Programs are offered: Trail Blazers for fathers and sons; Trail Mates for fathers and daughters; Trail Maidens for mothers and daughters; and Coed Trail Blazers for either fathers or mothers and their sons or daughters.

YMCA Trail Programs have been developed out of a concern for families. The family is the major support group for most of us: It is the place where values are developed, where we learn to care and express love, where we discover our strengths and weaknesses, and where we are accepted for what we are.

Through Trail Programs, the YMCA provides opportunities for families to enjoy themselves, to spend quality time together, and to experience an environment in which parent-child communication and growth can freely take place. Because strong individuals build strong families, Y-Trail Programs are designed to concentrate on the relationship between an individual youth and his or her parents.

For many parents and children, participation in Y-Trail Programs will follow participation in Y-Indian Guide programs, although this is not necessary. Y-Indian Guide Programs are a cornerstone of core programs offered by most Ys for the family with elementary-school-aged children. Trail Programs focus on strengthening the parent/child teams. The focus is on children from fourth grade up, even well into junior high school, with emphasis shifting to the child's skill development, leadership, and accomplishments with the support of the parent.

In YMCA programs, our first commitment is

to the personal development of each participant. We seek in all programs to help participants develop values, improve personal relationships, appreciate diversity, become better leaders and supporters, develop specific skills, and have *fun*.

Basic Information

The following are some of the basic goals and terms of the Y-Trail Programs:

- **The aim** of the programs is to enrich the companionship and relationship of parents and children as they explore their environment, community, and lives together.
- **The focus** is primarily on children 9 to 11 years of age (fourth, fifth, and sixth graders) and their parents in a team relationship. If they wish, children may continue participating as they grow older, even into their teens.
- **Membership** is open to all children in the upper elementary grades and their parents. Many will be coming from Y-Indian Guide units. Because the Y-Trail Programs are an integral part of the YMCA, all members of the programs must also become members of the local YMCA.
- **The group**, or club, is the basic organizational unit for Y-Trail Programs. Each group consists of 6 to 10 parent/child teams, and may be coed, particularly if the children are younger than 10. Activities appropriate for both boys and girls, as well as for the parents, are easily planned for this age group. For programs that include children older than 10, it is recommended that parent/son and parent/daughter groups be organized.
- **The Trail Council** is an intergroup organization that supports the program planning of each group, coordinates special Council events that include all groups, and establishes sound program practices. Council events provide opportunities for groups to meet and enjoy activities that are more suited to large numbers of people.
- **Meetings** of Y-Trail Programs are usually held twice a month. Most groups have found that it works best to spend one of these meetings at a member's home and the other pursuing some activity in the community. Some meetings can also be held at the YMCA.
- **The theme** is the central topic around which all activities are developed. The choice of theme should be based on local members' interests in such things as space, community exploration, early American history, or camping and outdoor recreation. The theme is determined by the local Trail Council.

History of Y-Trail Programs

Since the beginning of the YMCA Indian Guide Programs in 1926, a few groups every year have continued the significant parent/child group relationships initiated with the younger child programs. Such groups have been called Senior Y-Guides, Y-Warriors, Y-Adventure Guides, Y-Voyagers, Y-Rangers, Y-Pathfinders, and Father and Son Gra-Y. Based on the work of several task forces and the field testing of many different models, the name of Y-Trail Blazers was chosen for the program in 1969. As the number of Indian Guide Programs for younger children grew with the addition of Maidens (mother/daughter), Princesses (father/daughter), and Braves (mother/son), so did the need for older child programs that would follow the pattern of the younger child programs. In the past several years, many different formats and themes have proved to be successful. This manual is the result of a need to combine in one resource the best activities, methods, and techniques that have been used with success in the older child programs during the past years of the programs' existence.

Differences Between Indian Guide and Trail Programs

Trail Programs normally start when a child reaches 9 years of age, although some children start at 10 or 11. In the Indian Guide Program, most of the planning and decision making is done by the parents. Because of the short attention span of children under the age of 9, activities are many and varied. Most children at the age of 9, however, are entering a new stage of development, and the Trail Programs are designed to take advantage of the growth opportunities that exist during this period of life.

One important goal of the program is to involve the older child in decision making, program planning, and leadership. Children can be given a primary role in designing the programs and carrying them out while parents provide important emotional support and help with decision making and problem solving. Looking at options, considering consequences, making decisions, and acting on those decisions are skills that children this age can learn with the guidance of their parents. This learning process also helps older children to develop and practice the skills of leadership and the social skills involved in relating to others their own age. Recognizing that older children are able to assist in the planning but are still willing to accept the suggestions and approval of adults is crucial to the success of a Trail Program.

The activities of Trail Programs are a bit different from those of the Guide Programs. Simple camping and outdoor activities give way to more challenging activities, such as the following:

Cave exploring
Canoeing
Surfing
Gun safety
Snorkeling

Backpacking
Rock climbing
Horseback riding
Scuba diving
Snow skiing

Projects involving manual dexterity become more involved and often take more than one session to complete. The following list includes possibilities for such projects that are well-suited for group effort and that are also provided for in the awards program discussed later in this manual:

Ceramics
Rocket and airplane building
Photography
Bike repair
Cooking

Clock building
Farming
Sewing
Cross-stitch
Astronomy

At this age, children usually develop preferences for specific activities, and Trail Programs allow for this heightened interest. A broad variety of activities and interests is recommended for children who are still in their elementary years. As children enter the teen years, however, their interests may narrow to two or three specific areas in which they would like to develop their skills and abilities. Parents should understand and orchestrate this type of progression as activities are planned. Activities and experiences for older children should be based upon their needs to explore their community, meet interesting people, understand their peers, develop satisfying self-images as they move outside their home, and achieve a deepening love and respect for all members of their family.

Emblem

The national emblem for the Y-Trail Programs uses the colors red, silver, and yellow to denote the warm understanding, vital sharing, and deep loyalty in the parent/child relationship.

4   Introduction

The compass with the Y emblem at its center signifies the ideas and aims of the "Four Trails" toward which the parent/child companionship experience is directed: Wisdom, Physical Health, Spiritual Growth, and Service. The border enveloping the compass portrays the power and the bonds of family support that strengthen its individual members. Participants in the programs experience the fun and excitement of exploring new worlds of interest in a spirit of adventure. From this the emblem developed.

Themes

Themes can serve to strengthen and enhance participants' involvement in the program. A theme can become a focal point for developing activities and can provide a variety of experiences. In this section, we present a number of options, and suggest that the Trail Council decide on a theme best suited to its particular program and its members. Changing the theme as children grow older can be a way to maintain children's interest as well as to meet the need for progression in program planning.

Regardless of the option chosen, the theme can be a stimulus for developing activities. Costuming, crafts, projects, trips, guest resources, special events, and games are examples of the many different things that can be planned around a chosen theme.

Some theme options to consider include the following:

- *Town theme.* Organize the program around the idea of the basic group being the town and the Council being the territory. Officers can take on such roles as mayor and governor. Activities can be designed to aid the children in learning the roles that government officials play when administering the government.
- *Indian theme.* This theme is a continuation of the themes and related activities in Y-Indian Guide Programs.
- *Space theme.* Organize the program and activities around planets, galaxies, constellations, and so on.
- *Nautical theme.* Organize the program and activities around ships, reefs, captains, and other nautical motifs.
- *Western theme.* Organize the program around the idea of the basic group being an outfit, the Council being a bunkhouse, officers being foremen and wranglers, and so on.

- *Medieval theme.* Organize the program around knights, castles, and so on.
- *No theme.* Many groups have a beneficial experience in the program without using a theme.

Group Procedure and Officers

The organization and official procedures of Y-Trail Programs should be determined by each local group. Here are some recommendations, however, based on the successful experiences of many groups across the country.

- Group officers should be children who are elected on a rotating basis (say every six months). These officers may be appointed

by the parents the first time, but thereafter should be elected by the children. All of the officers suggested here are not necessary; some groups choose only a few.
- Many groups have a positive experience sharing responsibilities and avoiding the establishment of permanent officers.
- Parents may assist their children by sitting next to them to encourage, coach, and support them in their leadership and group roles.
- Parents are encouraged to meet at least quarterly. These meetings could include appraising what has happened in terms of group effectiveness and personal enjoyment. They could spend time learning more about their children's development and about their role as parents. A parent meeting also provides the opportunity for problem solving and discussion of new program possibilities to present to the children for further discussion and approval.
- The following is a list of suggested officers. Terminology and roles may vary based on theme, local tradition, and direction of participants.

Trail Guide/President: Presides at group sessions, checks with Trail Aide to review the next meeting's program plans, appoints chairs and committees to handle special projects or activities, and attends Council meetings with parent.

Trail Aide/Vice-President: Leads opening devotions and ritual, assists with meeting arrangements, is responsible for insuring that programs are set up at least one month in advance, and presides in the absence of the Trail Guide.

Note Taker/Secretary: Keeps a record of meetings, important decisions, and group adventures. Maintains roster of members and corresponds with the YMCA. (A sample roster can be found in the appendix.) The Note Taker also handles group correspondence when necessary.

Purse Keeper/Treasurer: Keeps clear and accurate records of group dues, funds, and expenses. Collects fees from group members and forwards them to the YMCA or appropriate location. The Purse Keeper is responsible for all financial transactions of the group.

Linesman/Telephone Coordinator: Coordinates phone calling. The Linesman's primary responsibility is to remind members of meetings as well as to advise them of any last-minute preparation needs or changes in plans.

Pathfinder/Chaplain: Serves as a chaplain for the group, occasionally preparing devotions, prayers, and so on.

Historian: Serves as the historian, or record keeper, of activities and events. This might involve keeping a scrapbook with pictures of group activities.

Awards Chair: Serves as the coordinator of the awards system if the group desires to be involved in a recognition program.

Transfer of leadership from the parents to the children needs to be planned carefully and implemented gradually in the fourth-, fifth-, and sixth-grade Trail Program groups. By the time some of the groups are in junior high or high school, the children are running the meetings completely by themselves. The parents' role needs to evolve into one of advisor, coach, listener, counselor, and supporter. Running meetings is also a good way to learn *Robert's Rules of Order*, available in bookstores.

Planning Chart or Calendar

Many groups have found charts or calendars useful in planning their group meetings or activities. A sample calendar can be found in the appendix. This calendar establishes well ahead of time responsibilities for hosting, projects, and other activities for the year.

Sample Meeting Outline

Here is a sample outline of a typical Y-Trail meeting:
OPENING

Trail Guide: "Will the (*name of Y*) Y-Trail (*Blazers/Mates/Maidens*) please come to order. Let our Trail Aide lead us in our opening ritual and meditation."

Trail Aide: "Y-Trail (*Blazers/Mates/Maidens*), what is your motto?"

Members: "Parent and child, blazing new trails together."

Trail Aide: "Y-Trail (*Blazers/Mates/Maidens*), what is your pledge?"

Members: "As a Y-Trail (*Blazer/Mate/Maiden*), my pledge is to strengthen the bonds of companionship with my (*father/mother/daughter/son*) as we explore our environment, our community, and our lives together, seeking to grow in spiritual, mental, and physical fitness, and in service to others."

Trail Aide: "You may be seated."

PATHFINDER'S MESSAGE The pathfinder delivers a prayer, scripture, story, or initiates a values activity about personal attitudes, behavior, or family life. A brief discussion may follow. The Pathfinder may also rotate this assignment among the other children in the group, and parents can be very helpful in preparation.

NOTE TAKER'S REPORT

PURSE KEEPER'S REPORT AND COLLECTION OF ANY MONIES

OLD BUSINESS

NEW BUSINESS

PROGRAM This is the heart of the meeting. Major attention, and most of the meeting's time, should be devoted to this item. Groups who have had experience planning meetings say that the key to the success of a program is fun. Many things are accomplished through the program, but *fun* should be a major goal.

REFRESHMENTS After an activity, light and simple refreshments can be served. At times the children like to prepare their favorite dessert.

CLOSING CIRCLE Parents and children stand in a circle, arm in arm, and repeat the following verse:

"And now may God
Be before us to guide us,
Beneath us to suppport us,
Behind us to forgive us,
And above us to bless us,
Now and always. Amen."

Chapter 2

Program and Group Planning Tools

Y-Trail Programs are developed and led by a combination of professional Y staff members and member parents and children. In this section we discuss various tools that they all can use in program planning and development.

Starting a Y-Trail Program

We suggest that one or two strong parent and child leaders who have participated in Indian Guide Programs initiate a Trail group. They will need to advertise and promote the Trail Program idea to the Indian Guide Program participants to obtain members. Advertising and promotion can also be done in places other then the Y such as schools, shopping malls, parades, churches, community bulletin boards, or any other place where potential members may be found.

After the program has been advertised, a meeting should be held for all prospective members to provide information about the program and attempt to interest both parents and children in joining. The following methods can be used:

Slide or video presentation	Make your own or use the one available from the YMCA Program Store.
Verbal presentation	Parents and children present some of their views of the program, emphasizing the fun they have had.

8 Program and Group Planning Tools

Campout presentation	Parents and children present ideas on weekend outings.
Outing presentation	Parents and children present ideas on outings, making sure to include outing ideas for the entire family.
YMCA involvement	The YMCA director presents his or her views of the program.
History	Present a history of the Indian Guide Programs, including the contributions of the founders, Harold Keltner and Joe Friday.
Handouts	Make available any type of handout necessary to create interest.

The list could go on and on. Above all, make sure that your presentation is an interesting one. Ask yourselves "What would we like to see and hear at one of these meetings?"

After the meeting, invite everyone to a Trail Program meeting to decide on officers, outings, meeting outlines, and the rules needed to run the program. (See the sample meeting outline on page 5.) Other sections in this manual may help with all this, such as "Brainstorming, Storyboarding, and Creativity" and "Facilitating Skills."

Keep in mind that this manual provides only suggestions; there can be other ways to conduct the program. This is what makes the Y-Trail Programs unique; you can tailor them to your own situation. What works for one group may not work for the other. We also suggest that attendance at national conventions and local workshops be a must to start any and all programs. Information on these can be obtained by contacting Program Services, YMCA of the USA, 101 N. Wacker, Chicago, IL 60606 or any of the five field offices.

Facilitating Skills

Many personal and social skills are learned in groups. How to solve problems, how to work with other people, how to communicate thoughts and feelings—these are just a few of the things that one learns in a group.

An effective group has the following qualities:

- Members clearly understand its purposes and goals.
- The group organization is flexible.
- Its members have a high degree of communication and understanding. Personal feelings and attitudes, as well as ideas, are handled in a direct and open fashion because they are considered important to the work of the group.
- Group members make decisions by carefully considering minority viewpoints and securing consensus on important decisions.
- Balance is maintained between group productivity and the satisfaction of individual needs.
- Members share leadership so that all can contribute ideas and can comment on the ideas of others, giving opinions and testing the usefulness of decisions.
- The group has a high degree of cohesiveness (members want to be together), but not to the point of stifling individual freedom.
- Members use their differing abilities intelligently.
- The group is not dominated by its leader or any of its members. The group can go

against the wishes of any member on occasion—no one person is the group.
- Members can objectively review their own methods of operation and adjust.
- A group can maintain a balance between emotional and rational behavior, channeling emotions into productive group effort.

Let's examine these characteristics and identify ways that you, as the program leader, can help your group become more effective.

Involvement Is Critical

An effective group works well when all members are actively involved, but this ideal doesn't just happen. It takes genuine effort and concentration to help people become involved.

There are a number of ways to stimulate members to take an active interest in the group:

- Spend time getting to know each member of the group yourself.
- Take time to let group members get to know each other. (You might structure activities during which the group can share information. Materials on values clarification and relationship building are available at the Y and at local libraries.)
- Before stating your own opinions, ask for other members' opinions on matters of importance to the group, either on a one-to-one basis or before the entire group. Don't say "I think that's a great idea, don't you?" When you state a question that way, you are not asking for their opinions; you are asking them to agree with you. Just say "What do you think?"
- Allow group members to make as many of the decisions that affect them as possible. (Again, don't say "I think we should skate, don't you?" but rather "Do you think we should skate?")

When you let children know that you value their ideas and feelings, they most often respond by becoming involved and taking responsibility. This, in turn, helps your group to become more effective.

Democracy, Autocracy, and You

At one time or another we have all been part of a group in which one leader dominated. That leader, often declaring that it was for the good of the group, dictated all activity. We may also have been part of a group with a designated leader who declined to lead and instead took the stance "Whatever you want to do is OK with me." Neither of these is very satisfying.

Decision is an important element of any group—what decisions the group makes, how it makes them, and who is involved. The key for your group is making sure that decisions are made appropriately. For example, some decisions affecting the group must be made by the program leader or even by a higher authority. If there is a fire in the building, one person must take charge. Other choices, like deciding what to do this afternoon, can best be made by those affected by the decision—the group members. In general, allow as much group input into decision making as possible. Children do know what they want and can make decisions for themselves, given appropriate guidelines and boundaries for the decisions.

Whenever possible, the feelings and ideas of every group member should be solicited before a decision is reached. This takes time and requires that you endure some frustration (not everyone will agree—some will simply want to be contrary). But if you value the ideas of group members and want the best decision, make the time.

Here are a few guidelines for choosing which process to use for decision making:

- Be *autocratic* (make the decision yourself without consulting the group) when there is an emergency or when no real choices exist for the group. For example, you might say, "It's time to get on the bus now so we will be home on time."
- Use *majority rule* when there is a choice among only two or three alternatives, or when a quick decision must be made.
- Use *consensus* (and take as much time as necessary to secure substantial agreement of all group members) for major decisions that will affect the group.

In all cases, think about these principles:

- Take time to make decisions—allow enough time to do it right.
- Clearly identify who will make the final decision. (If you are asking for group

members' ideas to help you make the best decision, let them know that.)
- Allow group control whenever possible.
- Give the group proper ground rules when they are allowed to make a decision ("You may choose any game you want, as long as it's a quiet game").
- Solicit the opinion of every member to get the best decision.

Task and Maintenance

In every group, two levels of activity take place all the time no matter what the group is doing—playing a game, having a discussion, or making a decision. The first level is called "task activity." This level includes everything that is done to complete the task at hand, such as generating ideas, seeking and giving information, coordinating, keeping the group on track, evaluating ideas, and doing whatever work is necessary to complete the task. The second level is called "maintenance activity." This level includes everything that is done to maintain the effectiveness and harmony of the group. Maintenance activities include encouraging others, harmonizing (or bringing ideas together), moving the group along, and setting standards for the group. Simply stated, task activity has to do with *what* the group is trying to do, and maintenance with *how and why* the group is trying to do it.

Your role as program leader is largely a maintenance role for your group. It will be important for you sometimes to become involved in the task—to keep things moving and to make sure the kids have a good experience. But it is more important that you pay attention to the maintenance issues.

Here are some specifics on maintenance:
- Work at the same physical level as the group—if they are sitting on the floor, you sit on the floor too.
- Work hard to get everyone involved—ask for the ideas of quiet members.
- Suggest methods for achieving the goals or tasks identified by the group.
- Carefully observe the behavior of each individual in the group—try to understand how each reacts and what turns off that person's interest.
- Identify the feelings, both positive and negative, that the group generates as it works ("I don't think Tommy liked that idea. He began scowling when you suggested that").
- Let other group members give their opinions on issues or decisions before you give yours.
- Act as a model of good communication skills—restate the ideas of a speaker before you react to those ideas; make your points clearly and simply.
- Accentuate the positive—let group members know that you care about them and that you like what they are doing.
- Ask lots of questions to clarify the situation, to make sure everyone understands what is being said, and to let others know that you are listening carefully.

In general, then, your role as a program leader with a small group will be to help that group become effective and cohesive and to stay that way. By being a good maintenance person, you help the children and adults learn more about themselves and others. They will also learn more effective ways of living and working together.

An effective group not only makes its members feel good about being part of it, it also helps them learn ways to make other groups —their families, friends, and organizations— more effective as well. You can make a difference if you improve your ability to handle small groups.

Brainstorming, Storyboarding, and Creativity

Brainstorming is a popular technique that has

been used by small groups for years. As Trail groups plan their activities, they may find this technique helpful. In the brainstorming process, each member of a group is asked to think of ideas that relate to a chosen topic. Traditionally, brainstorming has been accomplished by having one person facilitate the group and chart the ideas on a large sheet of paper. In recent years, an alternative method, called *storyboarding*, has become popular. Storyboarding differs from brainstorming in that ideas are written on 3" x 5" cards so that they can be easily grouped.

Whichever method is used, the following brainstorming rules can be helpful:

- All ideas count.
- No judging or criticism of ideas is allowed.
- Hitch-hiking (building on someone else's idea) is OK.
- The more ideas, the better.

The group should be reminded of these rules before a brainstorming session begins. Start by going around the room so that everyone gets a chance to give one idea. To prevent duplication, each person should call out his or her idea. As group facilitator, write the ideas on a flip chart so that everyone can see them. If the group runs low on ideas, use some of the following questions to generate more:

- Think about our senses. Are there things we can do with sight, sound, taste, touch, or smell related to this activity?
- Let's all think like the children in the group: What did we enjoy doing when we were this age? Now think like the adults: What do you think adults would enjoy doing?
- Are there some themes that could help us think of additional ideas?
- What have we done—or heard of people doing—that could be added to or improved?

Once you feel the group has exhausted its flow of ideas, have everyone begin to sort out, discuss, and debate those ideas that they have already brainstormed. Because of the need at this point to refine ideas, the ground rules for brainstorming no longer apply. It is important, however, to explain to everyone in the group that there are no bad ideas—just the need to refine and narrow the list to those that are applicable and possible for the group to implement. Once you've done some combining and eliminating of ideas, you will need to use the democratic process described earlier to help your group reach some agreements.

Chapter 3
Child and Parent Development

With their deepening peer orientation, children ages 9 to 12 will often challenge leaders or make contradictory demands on adults. At times they want their parents to be skilled, knowledgeable, and proficient. More often, however, they want parents to stand back and let them develop and demonstrate their own abilities. The successful leader of a group of older children will be sensitive and secure enough to recognize when one response or the other is appropriate. Adults working with these children must learn to draw leadership from the group rather than attempt to provide it externally.

Developmental Tasks of 9- to 12-Year-Olds

When a child reaches the age of 9, he or she has reached a very special year. Age 9 is the beginning of a new stage of development, the prepuberty period, which continues until adolescence. At this age the child begins to become independent of the parent, and opportunities to give service to others increase in importance. Adults can influence a child and make suggestions, but most children want to do things for themselves at this age.

Lessons in social justice, fairness, moral values, and standards of behavior can be taught with lasting impact at this time. This is an ideal age to capitalize on the self-motivation that is inherent to this stage of development, when children are able to make their own plans but still are ready to accept parents' suggestions and approval. According to psychologist Erik H. Erickson (as cited in the 1982 YMCA publication *School Age Child Care*, "Programming with Children," p. 11), children who are elementary or junior high school age face two basic developmental tasks: acquiring a sense of industry and developing a sense of competency. Erickson claims that the child who does not gain sufficient feelings of productivity and capability during these years instead develops feelings of inferiority and inadequacy.

Following is an expanded list of developmental tasks children should take on at this time:

- Learning specific physical skills necessary for playing sports and games
- Building wholesome attitudes toward oneself
- Learning to get along with peers and win one's way with a group
- Learning and accepting appropriate masculine or feminine roles, as well as developing sensitivity to the needs of the opposite sex
- Developing fundamental skills in reading, writing, and calculating
- Developing concepts necessary for everyday living, including acquaintance with the adult world
- Developing conscience, morality, and a recognition of values with an increasing interest in fair play, justice, and a belief in the worth of all people
- Developing decision-making skills, linking values to both decisions and actions taken on those decisions
- Achieving personal independence and becoming an autonomous person able to plan and act independently of parents and other adults
- Responding to one's peer group but being able at the same time to rely on family and parents
- Developing attitudes toward social groups and community service, and enjoying making others happy, with a growing response to God's love
- Formulating a personal faith, and using the strength found in that faith to withstand challenges and trials

In summary, children ages 9 to 12 move from deep initial attachment to their homes and families to strong new associations with their peers. They are in a growth stage that is often characterized by the following:

- Strong desire for live-away experiences
- Desire to be with peers in groups, teams, and clubs
- Long interest spans and the patience to work for short-term goals
- Formation of cliques and friendships with their own sex and age groups
- Desire to make, do, and collect things
- Seeking status through excellence in skills and knowledge of grown-up things
- Competitiveness in team and individual activities
- Mischievousness and daring
- Concern with physical size and appearance
- A developing interest in boys for girls at the upper age level
- Ability to work and socialize in programs where responsibility for planning is shared

Parents should remember that no child will precisely fit these general descriptions. Each is maturing in a unique way and at a unique pace.

A Word About the Teen Years

Many participants entering the teen years continue in Y-Trail Programs. They are experiencing a time in their lives that is flooded with various feelings. For many it is a time of real challenge. The pressure to be accepted, to do well in school and in other endeavors, to get along with parents, and to be attractive to the opposite sex creates a great deal of stress for a youth going through the early teen years. There are for teenagers, as there are for adults, times of great exhilaration and great depression; but some researchers suggest that teens often have higher highs and lower lows than adults do. The time spent in either of these, however, is less than adults might spend. Changes in anatomy and body chemistry further complicate the lives of teenagers.

Parents have an important, although different, role to play during the teen years. A challenge for adults trying to communicate with teens is to know when the teens want parent involvement and when they do not. Far more patience is required at this stage than at any other time in earlier years and parents need to avoid, as often as possible, causing feelings of insecurity and inadequacy in their child. It's important at this time for adults to be with other adults and to talk about parenting. Abundant information is also available through churches, social service agencies, and local libraries on issues that surface during the teen years. Parents should remember, above all, that parent support is a blessing for teens. While teens may not show appreciation, they desperately need to feel that they are loved for who they are, and not for what they do or don't do. Teens, although many would not admit it, look to parents for guidance. Setting guidelines together with your teen, and then monitoring those guidelines appropriately, can ease tension and prevent misunderstandings. These years mean more opportunities for teens, but also more responsibility. The guidance and understanding of parents at this time is crucial.

Chapter 4

Activities

This section of the manual is devoted to ideas for activities that form the core of parent/child experiences in the YMCA Trail Programs. Program activities must be more than a collection of fun gimmicks; they should enable both parent and child to achieve new insights and skills during this period. Balance and variety in program activities are essential to meet all participants' interests and needs.

Flexibility, rather than uniformity and rigidity, will characterize the best program experiences. The sample meeting outline and sample calendar of council events mentioned earlier are based on the activities found in this chapter: group meetings, family activities, outings, special interest group meetings, and parent/child communication activities. Many trail groups have found the themes of physical fitness, wisdom, spiritual growth, and service to others—along with fun—a real help in developing activities for group participants and their families.

Group Meetings

The following are suggested activities for group development and planning.

Show and Tell Programs

Pet night   Hobby night
Talent night   Recipe swap
Movie or slide night   Songfest
Riddle and joke night

Other Programs of Interest

Board game night
Charade or stunt night
Holiday celebrations
Impromptu drama
Novelty exercises or relays
Working on personal achievement award

17

18 Activities

Producing a home movie or slide show

Quiz sessions: Trivial Pursuit, mystery stunts, spelling bees

Parent surprise/youth surprise night—either the parents or the children prepare for the meeting, not letting the others know what is planned

Scavenger hunt or treasure hunt

Sports—kickball, backyard volleyball, badminton, croquet, softball, Jarts (lawn darts), bicycling, and touch football

Guest speakers—on computers, photography, fitness, law enforcement, bicycle safety, wilderness survival, pet care, or nutrition

Service Projects

Clean-up day at the YMCA or at parks

Mitten tree—collectible mittens contributed to youth home or charitable group

Nursing home visits

American Indian needs—such as Sioux Indian YMCA or Native American Outreach Project (Information on these can be obtained from the National YMCA.)

Car washes, paper drives, bake sales with proceeds donated to the above (or other) charities

Family Activities

These activities provide opportunities for the entire family to become involved in Y-Trail Programs.

Dinners

Barbecues	Potlucks
Progressive dinners	Backyard picnics

Special Interest

Circus	Pioneering
Crafts festival	Talent night
Canoeing	Swap meet
Puppet show	Family trace (tracing family trees)
Road rally	
Service projects	
Carnival	

Parties

Movie night	Holiday celebration
Pumpkin carving	Costume
Beach	Unbirthday

Physical Activities

Square dancing	Roller skating
Bowling	Fitness night
Miniature golf	Marble tournament
Swimming	

Outings

These trips and activities in the community offer fun for Y-Trail Program participants with families or as a group.

Trips

Amusement parks	Police or fire departments
Movie theatres	
Zoos	Hospitals
Planetariums	Factories
Symphony or orchestra concerts	Parents' places of employment
Museums	Restaurants
Water and sewer departments	Hayrides
Military bases	Mystery trips
Historic sites	Airports
Universities	Farms

Activities

Go-carting
Hiking
Fishing
Miniature golfing
Camping
Horseback riding
Fruit picking
Kite flying
Cycling
Cooking out
Tobogganing
Sledding
Ice skating
Staying overnight at the Y

Special Interest Group Meetings

As Trail Program groups develop through their first or second year, some participants might become interested in establishing one or two subgroups with a special focus. This special focus would allow participants to stay involved with a topic for a longer period of time than one meeting would allow. The focus group might last for four or more in-home meetings, with additional work between the meetings possible. Because of the specialized nature of the focus group activities, it is advisable to select a resource person familiar with the group's topic (possibly from outside the group) to provide the primary leadership throughout the multiple meeting involvement.

Here are some possible topics for focus groups:

Cave exploring
Photography
Model rocketry
Electronics
Community projects
Crime Prevention
Drug education
Astronomy
Marksmanship
Tennis
Cooking
Fishing
Square dancing
Model making
Survival training
CPR training
Bicycling
Team sports
Horseback riding
Gymnastics
Self-defense
Rappeling

Keep in mind the following suggestions for focus group development:

- An outside resource person can be helpful.
- Focus group activities may relate to the requirements for the awards programs, if desired.
- Focus group activities must be planned ahead so that each of the meetings is more challenging than the one before.
- Activities should emphasize learning by doing, using normal safety precautions.

Parent/Child Communication Activities

Information on parent/child communication activities is already available through a variety of resources. Ask your YMCA for copies of family program materials that contain some excellent discussion activities. YMCA program materials that might be helpful include Home Team resources, *School Age Child Care*, and *Vital Signs of Family Life*. In addition to these, your local bookstore or library will carry resources that could be helpful in giving you some ideas about parent/child communication activities. You might also like the Ungame board game.

Chapter 5

Recognition and Awards

Recognition is an important facet of the healthy growth of children and parents. Awards, if used in the Y-Trail Programs, should be available to all. They should emphasize personal growth and achievements, service to others, and full support of the Trail group's activities. They are not a requirement, and many individuals enjoy participating in the Y-Trail Programs without being involved in the awards program. Others find that the awards enhance their experience in the programs.

The best kind of motivation for participating and progressing in a program is intrinsic motivation—that is, motivation that arises when the activity produces inherent satisfaction and when the group provides worthwhile and enjoyable experiences to all its members. Artificial incentives, such as awards, should be minimized so that an award does not become an end in itself. Recognition of an individual's worth and progress should be shared sincerely and openly by all the parents and children in the group, and should be planned with care. Caution should be exercised against its potential misuse or overemphasis.

The National Award System

While recognition programs vary in nature among local YMCAs, there is a National Award System available that is used by many YMCAs. Awards are organized into the following six areas of achievement:

- History and Community (Green Group)
- Outdoors (Red Group)
- Sports (Blue Group)

22 Recognition and Awards

- Science, Nature, and Animals (Orange Group)
- Special Interests (Yellow Group)
- Health and Safety (Brown Group)

Within each color grouping is a variety of awards. Patches for each award are available through the YMCA Program Store. Parent/child teams earn awards by working on projects at home at their own pace. (Project ideas may be stimulated through demonstrations at regular group meetings.) Teams set their own goals, drawing upon the talents and resources of other teams. When projects are completed, they are reviewed by one or more examiners—adult experts designated by the Trail Council or YMCA Director.

Record Keeping, Monitoring, and Procedures

The following guidelines are a possible method of monitoring an awards system; local YMCAs may wish to develop their own method, using these guidelines as a starting point:

- Each child may work toward whichever award he or she chooses. Each parent is expected to work with his or her child as they both learn the requirements for a given award.
- Each award should have its own adult expert or examiner. This may be a person in the same Trail group, a parent from another Trail group, or an outside resource person who has volunteered to serve in the adult expert role. The adult expert is responsible for providing the training and resource materials necessary for teaching the requirements of that award. He or she may choose to teach the children as a group or individually and may teach separate requirements at separate times, as appropriate.
- Some awards are easily taught to the group by the adult expert. Other awards can more easily be completed on a parent/child basis and be certified by that parent. The method used is the parent's choice.
- An individual record for an award should be completed by either the adult expert or the parent, as appropriate. The original of this record should be given to the Awards Chair in the group as a permanent group record.
- All requirements for a given award should be successfully completed within a nine-month period.
- The Awards Chair of each group is responsible for the following: seeing that each award has an adult expert, administering the necessary records, keeping inventory of award patches, ordering award patches, and arranging the presentation of awards in an appropriate ceremony.

We want you to keep in mind that these are suggestions only. Each group may wish to use its own ideas when implementing the award system.

Award Requirements

This section describes the projects required to earn each of the awards in the National Award System.

History and Civic Awards—Green Group	
Anti-Litter	Home Citizenship
Community Citizenship	Indian Lore
	National Citizenship
Flag	Natural Resources
Geography	

Anti-Litter Award— Green Group

Purpose
To create awareness and personal concern about the environment.

Requirements
1. Read a newspaper article, magazine article, or book on the subject of pollution, conservation, litter, vandalism, or solid waste disposal.
2. Find the addresses and hours of operation of collection points for metal cans, glass bottles, and paper in the local community.
3. Spend a minimum of three hours gathering litter on roadsides, trails, campsites, and public lands and dispose of it properly (suggested as a group project).
4. Pledge to help keep the land clean and free of litter, and try to leave every campsite used by Y-Trail Programs more litter-free than when you found it.

Community Citizenship Award—Green Group

Purpose
To better understand the community and how it helps people who live there.

Requirements
1. Describe briefly how your community (town, city, or local area) was founded, how it was named, its historical events, and something about the people who contributed prominently to its growth.
2. On a map of your community, point out the following:
   a. Nearest fire station, police station, hospital, schools, churches
   b. Important government buildings
   c. Railroad and bus stations and airports
   d. Main highways
   e. Public recreation area near where you live
3. Visit a newspaper publishing company, radio station, or television station to learn how it keeps your community informed. Tell why it is important.
4. Tell how to do the following in your community:
   a. Report a fire.
   b. Report an automobile accident.
   c. Call an ambulance.
   d. Report damage to the electric power, gas, or water supply system.
   e. Register your bicycle.
5. Visit one department of your local government and report on the services that it provides to your community.
6. Describe briefly the work of three volunteer organizations in which people of your community work together for the general welfare.
7. Plan a community service project that will require at least two hours of your time.

Flag Award—Green Group

Purpose
To learn the proper use and care of the flag of the United States of America.

Requirements
1. Tell when a flag should be displayed.
2. Tell how to display flags of two or more nations.
3. Tell how to hang an American flag on a wall or above a street.
4. Tell when a flag may be used as a cover or drapery.
5. Demonstrate the proper way to fold a flag.
6. Tell how to show proper respect for the flag when it passes.
7. Tell how to dispose of a worn flag.
8. Tell the proper procedure for raising and lowering the flag on a pole, including half-mast.
9. Give a brief history of the American flag.

Geography Award— Green Group

Purpose
To learn the states and important areas of your country.

Requirements
1. Be able to name and identify all 50 states on a blank map that has state boundaries only.
2. Be able to name and identify the five Great Lakes, the Mississippi River, the Ohio River, the Missouri River, the Atlantic Ocean, the Pacific Ocean, and the Gulf of Mexico.
3. On a map, locate the Rocky Mountains, Great Plains, Appalachian Mountains, Sierra-Nevada Mountains, a desert area, and a tropic area.
4. Tell about your state and the location of its important rivers, mountains, and lakes.
5. Take a field trip to a state park or state forest, and later describe what you saw.

Home Citizenship Award— Green Group

Purpose
To develop a better understanding of home citizenship.

Requirements
1. Discuss the meaning of citizenship and the importance of your home in your training for citizenship.
2. Practice good citizenship at home by being courteous, fair, and helpful to other members of your family.
3. Keep a one-month record of at least five regular home chores, showing how often you do them.
4. Make a budget and keep a record of your own income and expenses for two months.
5. Earn the Home Safety Award.
6. Tell how to get help in case of accident, illness, fire, and other emergencies in your home.
7. Help plan, prepare for, and carry out a family group activity and give a report.

Indian Lore Award— Green Group

Purpose
To learn the history of our American Indian tribes.

Requirements
1. Visit a historical American Indian site (preferably in your own state) and learn the history of the tribe that lived there.
2. Give a report to your group on this visit, and include the history of both the site and the tribe. Your report should also include the following:
    a. Type of dwellings the tribe lived in
    b. Foods they ate and how they prepared them
    c. Nature of the life they lived (hunting, farming, etc.)
    d. Their religious beliefs
    e. Major class of Indians they belonged to, and the language they spoke
3. Do at least six of the following:
    a. Make an American Indian costume. Try to make the costume authentic and complete.
    b. Take part in an Indian ceremony.
    c. Sing two Indian songs in an Indian language and explain their meaning.
    d. Perform two Indian dances and explain their meaning.
    e. Learn at least 25 common terms in Indian dialect or sign language.
    f. Learn two Indian games and lead one with your group.
    g. Make an authentic model of an Indian dwelling.
    h. Learn and demonstrate Indian cooking. Cook at least two dishes.
    i. Name six famous Indian chiefs, and tell which tribes they were from and why they were famous.
    j. Tell your group at least one Indian legend. (A legend should require at least five minutes to tell.)
    k. On a former Indian site, collect at least five Indian artifacts and identify them.

National Citizenship Award—Green Group

Purpose
To develop a better understanding of one's citizenship.

Requirements
1. Read the Declaration of Independence and briefly explain what it means.

2. Read the Constitution of the United States of America with its amendments and do the following:
   a. Briefly explain its purpose.
   b. Describe the three branches of government and the system of checks and balances.
   c. Tell how the Constitution may be amended.
3. The privileges in our Bill of Rights have been protected in our country, but in some other countries they have been denied. Give two examples where they have been denied, preferably from news articles.
4. Visit your national or state capital, a federal project that serves your community, or a place that figured in the history of our nation, and give a report to your group.
5. Tell the names of the senators from your state and the representative from your district in Congress. Show how to properly address a letter to one of them.
6. Describe five ways in which the federal government serves you, your family, and your community directly.

Natural Resources Award—Green Group

Purpose
To learn about the natural resources of your country and your state.

Requirements
1. On a map of the United States, indicate areas that produce oil, coal, timber, gold, iron ore, limestone, corn, wheat, cotton, cattle, fruit, and dairy products.
2. Tell where five things in your home are made.
3. Draw a simple map of your state and indicate important areas for food production, raw material sources, and manufacturing.
4. Tell of any natural resources that are important to your state.
5. Take a field trip to a mine, quarry, or other natural resource and describe what you saw there.

Outdoor Awards—Red Group	
Backpacking	Firebuilding
Camping	Fishing
Canoeing	Hiking
Compass	Outdoor Cooking

Backpacking Award—Red Group

Purpose
To learn the proper way to prepare for an overnight hike.

Requirements
1. Prepare a list of the necessary equipment.
2. Prepare a menu and list the foods needed for this menu.
3. Secure appropriate maps and plan your route.
4. Properly pack your own pack, roll your own sleeping bag, and carry your share of equipment and food.
5. Hike at least 1½ miles and sleep overnight.
6. Assist in building the campfire and preparing the meals.
7. Use the proper method to put out your campfire before moving on.
8. Describe four types of packs and the advantages and disadvantages of each.

Camping Award—Red Group

Purpose
To practice the skills of an all-around camper.

Requirements
1. Complete the following awards:
   a. Knife and Axe Safety
   b. Compass
   c. Firebuilding
   d. Knot Tying
   e. Outdoor Cooking
2. Select and prepare a campsite. Tell why you chose that site.
3. Spend at least one night in the campsite.

4. Accumulate a minimum of 10 nights of camping.
5. Explain what precautions are necessary for clean drinking water, sanitary facilities, and emergencies.
6. Explain how and why weather, season, and water supply must be considered when planning a campout.

Canoe Award—Red Group

Purpose
To learn how to handle a canoe with enough skill to take a one-day canoe trip.

Requirements
1. Complete the Advanced Swimming Award.
2. Demonstrate with your parent the following skills:
   a. Boarding and casting off
   b. Use of safety equipment
   c. Pivot turns to port and starboard
   d. Landing, debarking, and mooring the canoe
3. Know and identify the parts of a canoe. Show how to properly use a paddle.
4. Demonstrate what to do in case of an upset.
5. Tell how to keep a canoe in good condition.
6. Tell about the importance of checking weather conditions before canoeing.
7. Plan and execute with your parent a one-day canoe trip of at least 10 miles.

Compass Award—Red Group

Purpose
To provide a basic understanding of the compass and its use in conjunction with maps.

Requirements
1. Give the 16 points of the compass in proper order starting with North.
2. Describe the difference between magnetic North as shown on the compass and true North.
3. Show how to use a map and a compass to follow an indicated route.
4. Describe how a compass works.
5. Demonstrate how to travel continuously in a given magnetic direction from a magnetic compass reading.

Firebuilding Award—Red Group

Purpose
To learn how to build, use, and put out a campfire.

Requirements
1. Complete the Knife and Axe Safety Award.
2. Explain how to prepare an area before building a fire.
3. Be prepared to start and maintain a fire properly with matches, tinder, knife, and axe.
4. Explain how to extinguish a fire both with and without water.
5. Explain how to find dry tinder in the woods.
6. Make a fireplace of stones suitable for heating water or cooking.
7. Explain and demonstrate how to build a fire for cooking and a fire for warmth.

Fishing Award—Red Group

Purpose
To learn the basics of sport fishing.

Requirements
1. Name two ways that Indians caught fish.
2. Be able to identify the fishing laws in your state concerning age limits, type and size of fish, and number of fish allowed per catch.
3. Describe the proper fishing equipment for river or lake fishing.
4. Catch three different fish with your equipment and describe the kind of bait you used. Explain why you chose your equipment.
5. Name five kinds of fish found in the lakes and streams near your home.
6. Explain what to do if you hook yourself.
7. Find and identify three kinds of live bait.

Hiking Award—Red Group

Purpose
To learn how to prepare for hiking.

Requirements
1. Explain what precautions must be taken for safe hiking regarding equipment and terrain.
2. Secure a map of the area that you plan to hike in and lay out a trail to follow.
3. Prepare a time schedule for your hike. If the hike lasts over mealtime, prepare a menu.
4. Take a hike of at least 5 miles. Use the items mentioned in number 2 and number 3 above to prepare for the hike.
5. Take a hike of at least 10 miles, again using a map and a time schedule to prepare for the hike.

Outdoor Cooking Award—Red Group

Purpose
To learn how to plan and prepare outdoor meals.

Requirements
1. Familiarize yourself with basic outdoor utensils and cooking methods.
2. Demonstrate at least four types of outdoor cooking setups using wood as fuel.
3. Demonstrate a field kitchen setup using either a propane or liquid gas fuel stove.
4. Plan breakfast, dinner, and supper meals for you and your parent, and others, if you wish.
5. Shop for food, pack food, and describe how to take care of food at the campsite.
6. Cook at least two meals outdoors for you and your parent.
7. Wash, dry, and put away cooking utensils following the meals.

Sports Awards—Blue Group

Advanced Beginner/Intermediate Swimming
Advanced Intermediate Swimming
Advanced Swimming
Archery
Bicycling
Boating
Team Sports
Water Skiing

Advanced Beginner/Intermediate Swimming Award—Blue Group

Purpose
To learn basic swimming skills and water safety.

Requirements
Successfully complete National YMCA skill requirements for the Minnow and Fish levels of the Progressive Swimming Program.

1. Minnow Tests (Advanced Beginner)
   a. Demonstrate the survival float for 3 minutes.
   b. Tread water for 1 minute in deep water using a scissors kick.
   c. Swim the front crawl for 20-25 yards without a float belt.
   d. Swim the back crawl continuously for 20-25 yards.
   e. Demonstrate turning from a front crawl to a back crawl, doing a back float, then turning from a back crawl to a front crawl.
   f. Perform a front dive.
2. Fish Tests (Intermediate)
   a. Demonstrate the survival float for 6 minutes.
   b. Tread water for several minutes and demonstrate the breaststroke kick plus two additional treading kicks.
   c. Do the breaststroke kick for 50 yards.
   d. Demonstrate a dolphin or butterfly kick.
   e. Swim the elementary backstroke for 50 yards.
   f. Swim the front crawl for 50 yards with rotary breathing.
   g. Swim the back crawl for 50 yards.

h. Demonstrate the following sequence: swimming on front, turning, swimming on back, treading water, and then continuing to swim.
i. Perform a front dive from a standing position on a 1-meter diving board.

Advanced Intermediate Swimming Award— Blue Group

Purpose
To develop swimming endurance and survival water safety skills.

Requirements
Successfully complete the National YMCA swimming skill requirements for the Flying Fish Program.

1. Demonstrate the survival float for 6 minutes.
2. Know personal health issues related to pool use.
3. Swim the butterfly stroke for 50 yards.
4. Demonstrate the breaststroke.
5. Swim 200 yards using a combination of the butterfly stroke, back crawl, breaststroke, and front crawl continuously and in sequence (the individual medley). Execute strong push-offs at the ends of the pool.
6. Incorporate open turns into an individual medley and perform open turns without stopping between strokes.
7. Cover at least three or four body lengths swimming entirely underwater, using a breaststroke or a combination stroke.
8. Understand the difference between adventure and danger and develop ground rules to limit risk.
9. Perform extension assists.
10. Understand YMCA Aquatic Safety and Lifeguard Training.
11. Discuss underwater search and demonstrate a walking search in murky water.
12. Demonstrate mouth-to-mouth resuscitation.

Advanced Swimming Award—Blue Group

Purpose
To provide preparatory skills for the YMCA lifesaving program and to develop competence in all swimming strokes.

Requirements
Successfully complete the National YMCA tests for the Shark Program.

1. Demonstrate the HELP (heat escape lessening posture) position for 10 minutes.
2. Explain self-help procedures for exposure to the cold and for heat exhaustion.
3. Demonstrate the proper start from the edge of the pool and from the starting block at the deep end of the pool.
4. Demonstrate a properly executed breaststroke underwater from the start and on the turn.
5. Perform a front flip turn for the crawl stroke properly.
6. Demonstrate the back open turn.
7. Demonstrate the proper back crawl start and the back flip turn.
8. Swim the following lifesaving medley:
    a. 50 yards with the front crawl approach stroke
    b. 50 yards with the breaststroke approach
    c. 25 yards with the sidestroke on the left side
    d. 25 yards with the sidestroke on the right side
    e. 25 yards with the lifesaving stroke on the left side
    f. 25 yards with the lifesaving stroke on the right side
    g. 50 yards with the elementary backstroke
9. Perform a feet-first surface dive in 6 to 8 feet of water.
10. Perform a back dive off the diving board.
11. Know the symptoms of heat stroke and frostbite and how to treat them. Know how to avoid these problems.
12. Demonstrate an ice rescue and explain ice rescue skills.
13. Know the symptoms and the basic treatment of shock.
14. Demonstrate mouth-to-mouth resuscitation and know three special precautions to take in performing resuscitation.

Recognition and Awards

Archery Award—Blue Group

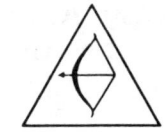

Purpose
To learn archery safety and the basic methods of using a bow.

Requirements
1. Explain bow safety.
2. Give the proper terminology for the necessary equipment and tell how each piece is used.
3. String and unstring a bow properly.
4. Using proper stance and pull, show how to shoot a bow.
5. At a distance of 30 feet, place 5 out of 10 arrows in a 3-foot round target.

Bicycling Award—Blue Group

Purpose
To learn bicycle safety and the rules of the road.

Requirements
1. Earn Bicycle Safety Award—Brown Group.
2. Earn Bicycle Care Award—Yellow Group.
3. Plan and execute at least three 10-mile trips covering city and/or rural routes.

Boating Award—Blue Group

Purpose
To learn boating safety and rowing skills.

Requirements
1. Know water and boating safety rules, including the use of safety equipment.
2. Identify and explain the use of the equipment necessary to row a boat.
3. Demonstrate the ability to row in a straight line for a distance of 100 feet.
4. Demonstrate the ability to turn right and left and to back up.
5. Demonstrate proper docking.
6. Know the various kinds of boats and the uses of each.
7. Build a scale model of a boat. (You may use a kit.)
8. Identify the different parts of a boat.

Team Sports Award—Blue Group

Purpose
To encourage the practice of sportsmanship and fair play.

Requirements
1. Participate on a team in any sport of your choice for one season, for example, a Gra-Y team of any sport, a summer soccer league, or Little League baseball.
2. In the sport of your choice and participation, explain the rules and scoring of the game.

Water Skiing Award—Blue Group

Purpose
To learn water skiing safety and how to water ski.

Requirements
1. Earn the Advanced Swimming Award. (This is mandatory.)
2. Know water and boating safety rules, including use of safety equipment.
3. Identify and explain the use of the equipment necessary to water ski.
4. Ski a distance of 100 yards.

30 Recognition and Awards

Science, Nature, and Animal Awards—Orange Group	
Astronomy	Reptile
Flower	Tree
Fossil	Weed
Geology	Wild Animal
Insect	Wild Bird
Pet	

Astronomy Award—Orange Group

Purpose
To increase knowledge of the universe and learn how to use the stars for location and direction.

Requirements
1. Locate and point out to the group the Big Dipper, Polaris, and four other constellations or planets.
2. Demonstrate the ability to determine true North by use of the stars.
3. Visit a planetarium and give a report on what you learned there.
4. Explain to the group how a telescope works.
5. Explain the difference between a planet and a star.

Flower Award—Orange Group

Purpose
To learn how to identify, plant, raise, and display flowers.

Requirements
1. Know at least 12 flowers, shrubs, or flowering trees.
2. Know at least six wildflowers.
3. Grow at least three kinds of flowers from seeds, plants, cuttings, or bulbs.
4. Visit a flower garden, greenhouse, or flower shop.
5. Go on a field trip to study wildflowers.
6. Make a flower notebook.
7. Give a talk to the group on flowers and display your flower notebook.

Fossil Award—Orange Group

Purpose
To learn about fossils and their place in the evolution of the earth.

Requirements
1. Explain briefly what fossils are and how they are found.
2. Name, and give the approximate age of, at least five periods in which the plants and animals that became fossils were alive.
3. Name at least five specific locations in your state where fossils can be found.
4. Take a field trip to at least one of these locations to collect fossils.
5. Make a display of at least 10 different fossils; describe to the group what they are and what period they are from.

Geology Award—Orange Group

Purpose
To gain a basic knowledge of geology, including rocks, minerals, and soil.

Requirements
1. Define the following terms: rocks, minerals, sedimentary rocks.
2. Answer the following questions:
   a. What are sedimentary rocks?
   b. How is soil formed?
   c. What are the main uses of rocks?
3. Make a collection of at least 12 rock, mineral, and soil samples. Make a display board of these samples.
4. Give a talk to the group explaining the things you have learned, and show the display board.

Insect Award—Orange Group

Purpose
To learn about different kinds of insects and how they benefit humans.

Requirements
1. Define *insect*.

2. Know common local insects.
3. Make a display box collection of no fewer than 25 local insects, identifying and listing their characteristics in a separate folder.
4. Know the benefits and the harm of local insects to humans and to the environment.

Pet Award—Orange Group

Purpose
To learn how to care for and train your pet.

Requirements
1. Take care of your pet for at least a month, including proper shelter, food, and exercise.
2. Describe the illnesses your pet is subject to and the ways to protect it against these illnesses.
3. Know what to do when your pet is ill, what precautions to take until help is available, and how to give your pet medicine.
4. Explain how to care for a female pet before and after she has had her young. Know the kind of food the newborns need if natural food isn't available, the kind of nest or bed needed, and the proper way to housebreak the young, if necessary.
5. Demonstrate the right way to carry your pet. If your pet can be trained, learn how to train it.
6. Learn about an organization or society that protects animals, or visit an animal shelter.
7. Make a record of all the information you have relating to your pet—photos, sketches, inoculations, special treatments, and so on.

Reptile Award—Orange Group

Purpose
To learn about the different kinds of reptiles and their natural habitats.

Requirements
1. Define *reptile*.
2. Name the five groups that make up the reptile family.
3. List 10 kinds of snakes. Tell where they are found, what their eating habits are, where and when they sleep, which of them are poisonous and nonpoisonous (and how to tell the difference), and what trouble their physical structures might cause.
4. List 10 kinds of lizards. Give the same information that you gave on your 10 kinds of snakes.
5. List 10 kinds of turtles and give the same information that you gave on snakes and lizards.

Tree Award—Orange Group

Purpose
To learn about trees and the valuable part they play in the earth's life cycle.

Requirements
1. Know and identify at least 10 trees native to your state.
2. Make a leaf collection of at least 10 different kinds of leaves.
3. Learn how trees fit into the earth's natural life cycle.
4. Learn how to plant and care for trees.
5. Exhibit your leaf collection to the group and discuss what you have learned about trees.
6. Learn the two basic types of trees.
7. Explain how to tell the age of a tree.

Weed Award—Orange Group

Purpose
To learn about the different kinds of weeds, how to identify them, and what harm they cause.

Requirements
1. Complete the following items:
   a. Define a weed.
   b. Classify weeds according to whether they are annuals, biennials, or perennials.
   c. Explain how weeds are scattered.

d. List the ways in which weeds cause losses.
e. Name some general methods of weed control.
f. Give the four plant parts in a good plant specimen.
g. Name the problems that weed pollen causes.
h. Name weeds that cause skin irritation.
i. Name weeds that are plant parasites.
2. Make a notebook about weeds.
3. Exhibit your weed book to the group and discuss what you have learned about weeds.

Wild Animal Award—Orange Group

Purpose
To increase appreciation, enjoyment, and knowledge of wild animals. To learn how to identify them.

Requirements
1. Check out and read a library book on wild animals, or read articles about wild animals in your state.
2. Identify by sight or tracks at least 10 wild animals native to your state.
3. Give a short presentation to your group on what you have learned about wild animals. Be prepared to answer questions.
4. Name three or more species of animals that face extinction and tell what is being done to keep these species alive.
5. Which animals are considered pests and why? Name at least two.

Wild Bird Award—Orange Group

Purpose
To increase appreciation, enjoyment, and knowledge of wild birds. To learn how to help and attract wild birds by building birdhouses, birdfeeders, and birdbaths.

Requirements
1. Check out and read a library book on wild birds and how to construct birdhouses, birdfeeders, and birdbaths.
2. Build and install one or more birdhouses and a birdbath or birdfeeder.
3. Give a short talk about all you have learned about birds or about a particular species of bird.
4. Name five or more species of birds that face extinction. Tell what is being done to keep these species alive.
5. Identify at least five wild birds outdoors.
6. Tell what *banding* is and why birds are banded.
7. Explain how migratory birds know where to migrate and how they navigate.

Special Interest Awards—Yellow Group	
Bicycle Care	Music
Gardening	Photo Developing
Home Repairs	Photography
Indoor Cooking	Reading
Knot Tying	Sewing
Leathercraft	Woodworking
Metalworking	

Bicycle Care Award—Yellow Group

Purpose
To learn how to maintain and repair bicycles.

Requirements
1. Tell how to take care of the finish on a bicycle.
2. Remove and replace an inner tube after patching for a flat tire.
3. Properly remove and replace the front and rear wheels (for a single-speed bicycle only).
4. Adjust the handlebars and the seat to different positions.
5. Explain how to remove the steering neck, pedals, crank assembly, and fenders.
6. Explain how to remove and replace the chain and how to adjust its slack.
7. Properly lubricate a bicycle.
8. Explain how to protect a bike from theft.

Gardening Award—
Yellow Group

Purpose
To learn how to raise and harvest one fruit or vegetable for family use or for the market.

Requirements
1. Choose a vegetable or fruit to grow. Find out about it by reading, observing, and talking with others.
2. Take sole charge of your crop for one growing season. Make a plan for selecting and preparing the planting site and for planting and caring for the crop. Keep a record of all costs involved and of all care that you give the crop.
3. Describe the protection you give the crop from diseases and from insect, animal, and bird damage.
4. Describe the tools, equipment, and supplies you use.
5. Pick your crop when it is ready to harvest, and record the quantity you have produced.
6. Learn how to prepare your fruit or vegetable for eating.
7. Share some of your crop with a neighbor or a friend.
8. Determine the cost of the same item if you purchased it in the store.

Home Repairs Award—
Yellow Group

Purpose
To learn the basics of home repair.

Requirements
1. Know the location and understand the function of electric fuses and/or circuit breakers in your house.
2. Demonstrate the proper method of splicing wire to extend a cord on a lamp or other electrical device.
3. Install fluorescent and incandescent light bulbs.
4. Prepare a list of basic tools needed around the home.
5. Lubricate drawer guides, windows, door hinges, and so on.
6. Erect a shelf that will support a 25-pound weight.
7. Repair a screen.
8. Repair a leaky faucet or pipe joint.
9. Mend a piece of broken furniture.
10. Replace furnace filters.
11. Fill the water softener.
12. Fix a squeaky step or board.
13. Tighten drawer knobs or handles.
14. Help an adult replace a pane of glass.
15. Help to paint or wallpaper and clean up afterwards.

Indoor Cooking Award—
Yellow Group

Purpose
To learn how to plan and prepare meals.

Requirements
1. Prepare a list of the four basic food groups that has at least two items in each group and explain the importance of a balanced meal.
2. Familiarize yourself with basic cooking utensils and methods.
3. Plan breakfast, dinner, and supper meals for at least four people.
    a. Make a menu.
    b. Shop for food.
    c. Follow at least two recipes.
    d. Prepare and serve the meals.
    e. Clean up after the meals.
4. Prepare one dish and dessert using the oven.
5. Make a drawing to indicate the proper place setting for a table.
6. Wash, dry, and put away supper dishes for your family for one week.

Knot-Tying Award—
Yellow Group

Purpose
To learn basic knots and some of their uses.

Requirements
1. Read some books or articles that describe basic knots and their uses.
2. Demonstrate how to tie the following knots:
    a. Square knot
    b. Clove hitch
    c. Sheet bend, using two different sizes of rope

d. Bowline
   e. Two half-hitches
   f. Taut-line hitch
3. Whip the end of a rope.
4. Name at least three different types of rope material and the advantages and disadvantages of each.
5. Explain at least one use for each of the knots listed in number 2.

Leathercraft Award—Yellow Group

Purpose
To learn the basics of leathercraft and how to make a few of the basic tools.

Requirements
1. Identify four kinds of leather and some ways in which each is used.
2. Make four stamps. Use 20-penny spikes and file the heads to make these stamps. With a little imagination, you can make many different kinds.
3. Learn and demonstrate how to lace using the buttonhole stitch method.
4. Make an item, such as a belt, coin purse, key holder, or wallet, by tooling leather. Show how to trace a design and transfer it to leather.
5. Show how to dye leather and how to finish it after tooling.
6. Describe proper care of shoes and other leather items.

Metal Working Award—Yellow Group

Purpose
To learn basic tools and methods of metal working.

Requirements
1. Learn how to use, care for, and store the tools generally used in metal work (drill, files, vise, ballpeen hammer, metal saw, tin saw, tin snips, pliers, and soldering or welding equipment).
2. Explain how the properties of gold, silver, tin, copper, aluminum, brass, and pewter affect the choice of the metal you would use to make certain articles.
3. Design and make a simple metal article requiring drilling, cutting, filing, and soldering or welding. Clean and polish the item.
4. Show and explain how to use a bolt, nut washer, lock washer, sheet metal screw, and rivet.
5. Explain how to cut a metal screw or bolt without losing the threads.
6. Know the differences between drills and saws used for wood and those used for metal.
7. Explain shop safety and how to prevent eye injuries, cuts, and burns.

Music Award—Yellow Group

Purpose
To become familiar with different kinds of musical instruments and compositions.

Requirements
Complete number 1 and three of the next five.

1. Give examples of the role that music plays in our daily lives.
2. Name the four general groups of musical instruments and give examples of each.
3. Name and define four basic music groups.
4. Demonstrate a musical instrument and explain its function within a musical group.
5. Attend a musical performance and report your impressions.
6. Define the following terms: composer, arranger, conductor, choreographer, vocalist, soloist.

Photo Developing Award—Yellow Group

Purpose
To learn how to develop negatives and make prints.

Requirements
1. Develop at least one roll of film for negatives and make at least six different good contact prints or enlargements from these negatives (no Polaroid prints).
2. Explain the process and the equipment that you used in number 1.

Photography Award—
Yellow Group

Purpose
To learn about cameras.

Requirements
1. Explain how a camera operates, including the flash unit.
2. Demonstrate how to load and unload film.
3. Plan and take a series of eight pictures or more that tell a sequence story, or take a movie sequence.
4. Take two pictures outdoors and two pictures indoors with a flash unit. These pictures may be part of the requirement in number 3 above. (All pictures must be clear and recognizable to qualify for a photography award.)

Reading Award—
Yellow Group

Purpose
To learn how to use the library.

Requirements
1. Read at least six books within a year. These books should be appropriate to your grade level and must include at least one book from each of three of the following classifications—adventure, biography, travel, technology, science, history, fiction, poetry, the arts, or hobbies. Books must be approved by your examiner.
2. Write a report of at least 200 words on two of the books.
3. Give a three-minute report to your group on at least one of the books.
4. Have your own library card.
5. Explain how to use a card catalog file to find a book in a library.

Sewing Award—
Yellow Group

Purpose
To acquire basic skills of sewing by hand and machine.

Requirements
1. Choose two items to make: tea towel, blouse, four napkins, four place mats, tablecloths, skirt, or something for a meeting. Then collect items for a personal sewing box. Include shears, pins, needles, thread, tape measure, pincushions, thimble. Learn sizes and kinds of needles and thread and the proper way to use a sewing table.
2. Find different kinds of cotton and polyester cloth. Decide which can be laundered and which cannot. Choose the cloth that can be washed for the things you make.
3. Name the parts of a sewing machine. Show how to thread it and the proper way to use it. Practice stitching evenly.
4. Learn how to use a pattern book.
5. Do the following:
    a. Make a plain seam
    b. Finish seams by pinking
    c. Overcasting
    d. Edge stitching
    e. Running hem
    f. Hem, fringe, or bind an edge
    g. Sew on snaps and hooks and eyes
    h. Sew on button
    i. Prepare fabric for cutting
6. Complete the two items you decided on in number 1. Use the skills you have learned. Explain what you did well and what you need to improve on.
7. List projects you would like to do in the future for yourself, the group, or the community.

Woodworking Award—
Yellow Group

Purpose
To develop skill using basic woodworking tools and to apply this training to craft projects.

Requirements
1. To show that you know how to use tools, demonstrate the following techniques:
    a. Proper care and use of a handsaw and hammer
    b. Proper care and use of chisels and planes

36 Recognition and Awards

   c. Use of square measuring tapes
   d. How to make and ready plans
   e. Use of coping saw
   f. How to operate and care for two simple power tools (such as a drill or sander). Describe the safety precautions necessary for using these tools.
2. Develop a project. Draw a plan of it and have your examiner approve it as suitable for the woodworking award. Some sample projects are a shoeshine box, birdhouse, small table, or shoe shelves. Advice from a parent is all right, but you must complete the project on your own.
3. Demonstrate your knowledge of lumber:
   a. Keep a record of the kinds and sizes of material used in your project.
   b. Explain the difference between common and finished lumber and some ways in which each is used.
   c. Explain what the grain in wood is.
   d. Explain the differences between, and the uses of, hard and soft wood, and name three types of each.
4. Keep a record of nails, screws, and other hardware used on your project.
5. Demonstrate your knowledge of paints:
   a. Keep a record of the kinds of paint used on your project.
   b. Keep a record of the wood finish used on your project.

Health and Safety Awards—Brown Group	
Bicycle Safety	Knife and Axe Safety
First Aid	Physical Fitness
Gun Safety	Water and Ice Safety
Home Safety	

Bicycle Safety Award—Brown Group

Purpose
To learn how to ride a bicycle safely and how to use the rules of the road.

Requirements
1. Attend a bicycle safety course conducted by local authorities and obtain a certificate of completion.
   OR
2. Do the following:
   a. Show that you can do these things on a bike: start, stop, use the brakes to control speed, balance yourself easily, ride at slow speed, steer, circle, and give proper signals.
   b. Know and follow traffic rules. Know the parts of your bike and how to spot-check for safety. Know how to chain and lock your bike for safekeeping. Have your bike registered.
   c. Show how to carry gear or packages on your bike safely.
   d. Following all the rules in items a and b, complete a bicycle safety course, making all the proper stops and signals. (This is a good group project.)

First Aid Award—Brown Group

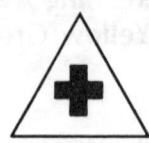

Purpose
To learn elementary first aid.

Requirements
1. Attend and pass a course conducted by an instructor who holds an advanced first aid card. Present to the group some of what you have learned in the course and present a suitable certificate signed by the instructor.

Gun Safety Award—Brown Group

Purpose
To learn the basics of handling a gun safely.

Requirements
1. Attend a gun safety class and earn your certificate.
2. Know the dangers of ammunition and explosives.
3. Know and demonstrate safe practices for the use of a gun.

Home Safety Award—Brown Group

Purpose

To learn and practice proper safety measures in the home.

Requirements
1. Know and follow the proper procedure for using and storing flammable or poisonous liquids and powders, matches, and medicine in your home.
2. Check your attic, basement, or utility room, and discuss with others what should be done in each to help keep the family safe and healthy.
3. List five common causes of fire in the home, along with steps for fire prevention. With your family, plan and practice a fire drill.
4. Using what you have learned, survey your home and yard and list any unsafe conditions; with the help of your family, correct as many of these conditions as you can.
5. Explain the proper use and care of wood and metal ladders.

Knife and Axe Safety Award—Brown Group

Purpose

To learn and practice the safe handling of knives and axes.

Requirements
1. Describe the uses of a knife and axe, and cite rules for safe handling.
2. Demonstrate the proper method of passing a knife and an axe to a buddy.
3. Demonstrate the proper method of sharpening a knife and an axe. Explain the importance of keeping the edges sharp.
4. Make a tent peg with an axe using the contact method.
5. Describe the proper way to store a knife or axe.
6. Explain what the Woodsman's Code means to you.

Woodsman's Code

I will use my sheath knife and axe as tools—not playthings.

I will keep them clean and sharp.

I will practice so that I may become skillful.

I will rest when tired and remember that "easy does it."

I will respect all safety rules to protect those about me.

I will respect the property of others and will not harm living things needlessly.

I will help others to live up to the Woodsman's Code.

Physical Fitness Award—Brown Group

Purpose

To encourage practice of physical fitness and exercise.

Requirements
1. Complete four of the following:
   a. Write a short paragraph on what physical fitness means to you.
   b. Write a short paragraph on the importance of brushing your teeth.
   c. Write a short paragraph on the harmful effects of tobacco, drugs, and alcohol.
   d. Write a short paragraph on the importance of keeping fit through a regular exercise program.
   e. Write a short paragraph on the importance of having yearly medical and dental examinations.
   f. Write a short paragraph on the importance of eating proper foods.
   g. Know how many hours of sleep are needed for children from 9 to 12 years of age. Explain why it is important to get good rest and sleep.
   h. Make a list of nutritious foods you would take on a two-day campout.
2. Keep a 30-day record of the following exercise routine:
   a. Neck rotators—Touch the chin to the chest, ears to the shoulders. Do

38 Recognition and Awards

15 circles. Reverse, turning to the right. Again do 15 circles.
  b. Toe touching—Bend over and touch the toes. Do not lock the knees. If you can't touch your toes, reach for your ankles. Repeat 25 times.
  c. Sit-ups—Lie on back with knees bent and hands interlocked behind neck. Curl up until lower back is at least perpendicular to the floor. Repeat as many times as possible, to a maximum of 50 times.
  d. Push-ups—Lie on stomach and push up with arms, keeping the back straight, to a maximum of 25 times.
  e. Running in place—Jog at the rate of 120 steps per minute. Run for as long as possible, to a maximum of 5 minutes.
  f. Skip a rope—Skip to a maximum of 3 minutes.
3. Compare the difference between the first three days of workouts and the last three days. Write a short paragraph about why you believe a change occurred.

Water and Ice Safety Award—Brown Group

Purpose
To learn basic safety around water and ice.

Requirements
1. Explain why the buddy system is good to use whenever you swim, ice skate, or go boating.
2. Demonstrate how to put on a life jacket correctly and explain why it is important to wear a life jacket in a boat.
3. Show how to get in and out of a boat safely.
4. With a companion, tip a boat or canoe, stay with it, and paddle 20 feet to shore while wearing the proper life jacket.
5. Without going in the water yourself, use a towel, pole, rope, or other object to help a tired swimmer.
6. Describe a couple of ways to rescue someone who has fallen through the ice.
7. Learn what to do if the ice is cracking under you.
8. Take a field trip to a frozen body of water and learn how to test the ice to see if it will hold your weight.

Chapter 6

Y-Trail Programs and the YMCA

The YMCA is an organization that is based upon the idea that "the members are the Association." Everyone who participates in a Y program is encouraged to take a leadership role and to become as active as he or she can in the support and operation of the Association. However, professional Y staff working with the Y-Trail Programs have special responsibilities. These include recruitment, training, supervision, and recognition of group leaders. Group leaders and Y staff form the basic leadership team for the program. Open and frequent communication is crucial.

Supported and attended by the YMCA staff, the regular meetings of the Trail Council focus on training, sharing, and planning. Group representatives can learn much at these meetings and also gain important support from each other and from staff who are trained in group work and family program skills.

In addition to their major roles in the Trail Council, the Y staff have special responsibilities to advise and support Council events and to develop support systems for the entire program (structure, promotion, registration, finances, evaluations).

Each YMCA across the country is operated independently by a local board that determines the programs and fees, including the fees for Y-Trail Programs. It may help to put costs into perspective by comparing benefits and costs among the YMCA Trail Programs, group athletics, and other local and national youth programs. Many Y programs are provided at fees that do not cover expenses. An important Y commitment is that no family be excluded from its programs because of inability to pay the fees. This philosophy demands a financial plan that obtains income from several different sources. These sources may include contributions raised during the YMCA annual current support campaign, allocations from United Way, special grants, and individual fees charged for the programs themselves. YMCA Trail Program members, leadership, and staff play an important role in ensuring the necessary financial support for this program.

The YMCA Trail Programs should be key programs at the YMCA. With the experience of participating in Trail Programs, many family members will become interested in other programs of the Y. In YMCAs across the country, millions of people have learned to swim and to play basketball, soccer, volleyball, and other team sports. Y day camp, resident camp, and trip camps are exciting for both youth and adults. Y preschool- and school-age child care provide a healthy environment for children and a feeling of security for their parents. All family members—moms, dads, uncles, aunts, and grandparents—enjoy Y fitness classes and many adults find Y pools a great place to maintain fitness.

Appendix

42 Appendix

Y-Trail Programs
Sample Planning Calendar

Group _____ Year _____

Participants	Sept 10	Sept 24	Oct 16	Oct 28	Nov 13	Nov 23	Dec 9	Dec 21	Jan 13	Jan 27	Feb 10	Feb 24	Mar 10	Mar 24	Apr 14	Apr 28	May 12	May 26	Jun 9	Jun 23
Atkins	H										H									
Price		H											H							
Butler				H										H						
Rodgers				H										H						
Bonney					H											H				
York															H					
Evans																H				
Hendrix								H										H		
VanLandingham							H											H		
Redmond										H										H

Column labels (vertical): Sept—PINNACLE MT. FAMILY PICNIC; Sept 24—HELFER PROJECT; Oct 16—MT. VIEW; Nov 13—TOLTEC MOUNDS; Nov 23—BICYCLE SAFETY; Dec 9—CAMPOUT; Dec 21—FAMILY NIGHT; Jan 13—HIKING TRIP; Jan 27—RICH CREEK; Feb—PLASTIC MODELS; Mar—GAS ENGINES; Apr—CAMPOUT; May—CANOE TRIP; Jun—LAKE OUACHITA

H = Host

Host is responsible for setting up meeting and calling others (if there is no Linesman officer). Children should help in the planning.

Council Events
September—Start Up Party
January—YMCA Overnight
April—Inter-Group Olympics
July—Family Festival

Y-Trail Programs Roster

Tr. guide _____   Group name _____   YMCA _____

Tr. leader _____   Roster date _____   Leader's phone _____

Names	Address (Street no., city, zip)	Phone Numbers	Spouse's Name
(P)		Home:	
(C)		Bus:	
(P)		Home:	
(C)		Bus:	
(P)		Home:	
(C)		Bus:	
(P)		Home:	
(C)		Bus:	
(P)		Home:	
(C)		Bus:	
(P)		Home:	
(C)		Bus:	
(P)		Home:	
(C)		Bus:	
(P)		Home:	
(C)		Bus:	
(P)		Home:	
(C)		Bus:	